FROM THE JAPANESE

Other books by Paul Rossiter:

In Daylight (Printed Matter Press, Yokohama/Sedona AZ, 1995)
Monumenta Nipponica (Saru Press, Tokyo, 1995)
The Painting Stick (Pine Wave Press, Sendai, 2005)

FROM THE JAPANESE

Paul Rossiter

ISOBAR
PRESS

First published in 2013 by

Isobar Press
Sakura 2-21-23-202
Setagaya-ku
Tokyo 156-0053
Japan

http://isobarpress.com

ISBN 978-4-907359-00-3

© Paul Rossiter, 2013
All rights reserved.

ACKNOWLEDGEMENTS

The cover photograph was taken by Kiyokawa Taiji in 1940 and is used by kind permission of Kiyokawa Mizue and the Setagaya Art Museum.

Earlier versions of some of the poems in Part II appeared in *In Daylight* (Printed Matter Press, 1995). Other poems and translations first appeared in *The Bow-Wow Shop, Edge, Poetry Tokyo* and *Printed Matter*. The translations by Arthur Binard and Kisaka Ryo were first published in *Gekkan Etegami* and *Kurosu Tooku*, and those by Natsuishi Ban'ya in *Ginyu*. My thanks to Arthur and Ryo, to Ban'ya, and to all the publishers and editors involved.

Contents

I

Basho	11
Reading Tu Fu in Tokyo, 1969	19
Club Mugen	20

II

Tokyo: Week One	23
Basho: Haiku	25
Komachi	26
Zuisenji Garden	28
Visiting Ian in Prison	29
Kogo, Scene 2	30
The Old Man of Shimo-Ochiai	33
Air / 空気	34
Some Cultural Uncertainties	36
A Small Bestiary	37
Bon-Odori in Kabukicho	38
Changing, Unchanged	39
Bow, Clap Twice, and Pray	40
Hokokuji	42
The Way of Tea	44
Kagekiyo	45
Hiroshima	48
From the Train	50
Ifu Beach, Kumejima	51

III

Vacuum Storm (*Natsuishi Ban'ya*)	55
Language Acquisition	58
The Old Lady of Ogikubo	59
Sashimi and Roses / 刺身と薔薇	60
A Letter from Ishinomaki	62
An Unseen Crow / 見えない鴉一羽	64

Notes   69

for Maya

I

1969

BASHO

after Matsuo Basho's Genjuan no Fu

1

Fifty years. My body, gnarled,
is an old tree which bears bitter peaches;
a larva with no cocoon,
a snail without a shell.
Wind-rift, cloud-drift, knowing
no destination, morning and evening
I have eaten traveller's fare
and held out my scrip for alms.

Last year, on my journey, my face
was burnt by the sun of Matsushima.
Skin taut and sore on my cheekbones,
I longed for that farthest shore
where puffins cry
and a thousand sea-scattered islands
can be seen from a steep northern cliff.

My companion held me back. Dangers
of the journey. Sickness. Age.

Bruised heels then, stumbling in dunes
on the rough northern coast, each step
a jolt to the bone, heels crunching grit.

But then this spring I wandered
alone by misty lake shores, reed-fledged
water's edge, looking for a place to rest,
a single stalk of reed
where a grebe's nest might be tethered,
might be borne by the current to rest.

Bamboo, brushwood, tall grasses,
a thatched hut abandoned deep in a thicket:
the crossroads of emptiness.

World-dust, crust
of cities, sifts away.

Rotting walls, damp thatch,
wrinkled bark on an aging tree,
tang of bitter fruit.

River-run, swift
        on sand. Rinse, sift
                by reeds, water's drift.

2

Few houses here where I have my hut –

a fragrant south wind from the heights,
north wind cool from the distant sea.

It was early summer when I came here,
azaleas blooming, mountain wisteria
hung from the pines. Cuckoos,
swallows' visits, the glance of wings.

Silence.
Tap of a woodpecker's beak on wood.

I called out to the wood dove:

> 'Come, bird of solitude,
> can't you provide a plaintive note?'

It was impossible not to be happy.

3

Clouded mountains, the pine of Karasaki,
wisps of mist, at times
a castle glimpsed amongst trees.
By the bridge over the shallow river
the hush and lisp of rain
quietens the waves of the lake,
the farther shore buried in mist.

Rain clears: peck of single drops
on wind-puckered lake water.
Tattered clouds. Late sunset lingers
in wet and scented pine groves,
damp brown needles beneath the quiet feet.

Mount Mikami looks like Fuji,
reminds me of my old cottage at its foot;
Mount Tanagami is haunted by the verses
of the ancients whose graves are on its slopes.

From time to time
I climb the peak behind my hut, and spread
a round straw mat on a pine bough shelf.

I call it my 'monkey's perch' –
and would never change it
for Hsü Ch'üan's drunken nest up a crab-apple tree,
nor for the hermit's hut
strung together by Wang the Sage.

I sit on the summit,
picking and crushing lice.

4

Now and then
I set out to gather firewood – dry
branches in awkward bundles,
a small man in a baggy half-coat
moving among the pines –

or draw spring water –

> clear drops
> trickling along the green
> of a single spray of fern.

Nothing weighs less than my stove.

5

A household shrine, an alcove
for hanging night clothes,
no other clutter from the man
who once lived here – just a plaque
with two words in a flowing hand:

> *Illusory*
> *Dwelling*

The calligrapher signed his name on the back –
a memento for those who might see it.

6

A passing traveller. My rush raincoat,
my broad-brimmed hat of nettlewood,
hang on a post above my pillow.

Daytime, and people come –

> villagers from the foot of the mountain
> (boars are grubbing the rice seedlings)
> or the old man from the shrine
> (rabbits are infesting the bean fields) –

and when, rarely, an old friend
comes on a visit from the distant city,
we sit at night
with the moonlight as our companion –

> hush of pines,
>   whisper of stars,
> distant waters'
>   ripple and lilt –

and argue quietly with our shadows.

7

Why do I live like this? Not because
I want to be a solitary in the wilderness
obliterating all my traces
with handfuls of dust. Rather, let's say
I'm an old man, in indifferent health,
grown weary of people . . .

What is there to say?

All my fifty years I've been a wanderer,
a man of strange ways, aimless
as the wind and clouds, and never
(although I've envied them, it's true)
the married man content with cities,
the official with his grant of lands –
nor even the monk who paces out his days
within the four strict walls of the Buddha's law.

But once I discovered I could make
my eccentricities a source of livelihood
(a passing whim of the world
I thought at first), I found my course set

and myself shackled for life
to the one horizon-bound line of my art.

Labour in vain:
wrinkled bark, bitter fruit.

8

Autumn is half over now:

> wind-rift,
> > cloud-drift
> morning, evening,
> > river-run, swift,

> a single stalk
> > of reed,
> of sedge, at
> > water's edge –

is there any dwelling on earth
which is not an illusory dwelling?

The thought goes, and I go to bed.

London, 1969

Reading Tu Fu in Tokyo, 1969

An autumn evening in the garden.
Moon rising, birds in their nests,
I sit among trees, alone.

Good now to play this white wood lute . . .
I lay the book aside and watch
the full moon start its climb behind the trees.

The distant clatter of a commuter train,
a police siren Dopplering and diminishing,
the ceaseless weave of traffic in Shibuya –

a faint rim of sound
around the outer edge of nightfall.
Meanwhile, not so far from here –

automatic weapons in their hands
and Hendrix pulsing in their heads –
squads of young draftees head back to base.

Burning villages, corpses in paddy fields,
refugees – Tu Fu had seen all that.
A sleepy chirp from somewhere

deep within the bamboo thicket.
Lute sounds linger, fading, cease –
autumn night, dark – that trembling leaf . . .

Club Mugen

I sit at the bar and drink
while music throbs and coloured lights
blink and blob and flash.

Sexy Suzy
sashays across the dance floor
and sits down beside me, laughing.

He thought, she says, *he was being big-time!
Five thousand yen!
I don't even take my eyelashes off for that!*

By the Gents
a GI borrows money from his buddy,
then crosses the floor towards us.

Here he is.
His fists are big.
You laughin' at me, kid?

It's the worm inside with dignity and teeth
that makes the scene I see,
the parts we play.

I never laugh, I say.

Tokyo 1969

II

1981-85

Tokyo: Week One

1

switches: up is on, down is off
each night I turn my key the wrong way in the lock

入口 = entrance
出口 = exit
板橋本町 = my subway stop

2

Shinjuku, Shibuya
neon bite and semiotic flash:

Italian pizza in a German beer hall
       where a dapper five-piece band
is playing *Dear Old Dixie*

a Jamaican ganja gangster film
       watched by intense young Japanese
in dreadlocks and Rastafarian hats

Scotch whisky in a plastic space-age bar
       my glass embossed
with a bust of Goethe, his name and dates

(a peaty nostalgia
       for what things 'really' mean
smoulders in the glass and on the tongue)

3

the first post arrives from England
familiar words
and familiar names on airmail paper
these too begin to slip away from what they meant

    six mats and a sliding door
    looking out across miles of rooftops
    to sunset behind Mount Fuji

loneliness, says Abe Kobo –
an unsatisfied thirst for illusion

    Ring Road 7 growls six floors below

this must be the place
a world of signs without fault
    without truth and without origin
the somewhere where meaning plays

September 1981

Basho: Haiku

look carefully
shepherd's purse
flowering in the hedge

this road
with no one going along it
autumn evening

winter seclusion
again adjust
my back to this door post

young sparrows
answering voices
a nest of baby mice

morning dew
dirty cool
muddy melon

lightning!
out of darkness
a night heron calls

Komachi

> *Ohta Shogo's* Komachi Fuden *performed by the Tenkei Gekijo Theatre Company*

an old woman is crossing a bridge by twilight
centimetre by centimetre she's approaching her death

a flock of ghosts shuffle behind her
her furniture stacked high on their backs

she steps off the bridge and sits down to rest
the ghosts assemble her house around her, then vanish

she sits like a *sotoba*, like a tree-stump, like a stone
among battered cupboards and torn paper screens

she cooks instant noodles on a small charcoal stove
it takes for ever, suddenly she slams a cupboard door

she winds up a gramophone and puts on Edith Piaf
an officer in whites appears and shimmers before her

the record ends, the suitor vanishes
the old woman eats her noodles

a doctor and a nurse tiptoe towards her
when they reach her they find that she's dead

the ghosts return and dismantle the house
a clumsy ballet of capering wardrobes and tables

now no one and nothing is here
except for an old woman and her gramophone

she will never move again – but then she stirs
she winds up the gramophone but no sound comes out

she moves to the bank of the river
and kneels at the edge of everything

she cups her hands and drinks
quenching solitude with knowledge of solitude

Zuisenji Garden

pool
black wind-ruffled water

an island
        two small bridges
a yellow sandstone cliff
a large shallow cave

dry winter season
        a brown gully
the memory of a waterfall

the garden is simply made up of two elements
rocks and water
this concealed beauty of the garden
enchants us very much

        unimpressive
        unexciting

sustaining
in its taste of nothing

absence of flavour which haunts the tongue

Visiting Ian in Prison

he's pale and thin and drawn
his arm in a sling

RULES OF THE PRISON:

> *don't escape*
> *don't kill yourself*
> *don't speak (and forty-six more)*

when I come out after an hour
I feel I've been inside for months

blue sky, an uncanny quietness
sunlight on white railings in the car park
salt wind, the tang of seaweed
a small stream rippling in a concrete channel

> sudden quenching
> of a thirst I didn't know I'd had

*'I haven't seen the sky for seven weeks
and the food comes in through a hole in the door'*

Kogo, Scene 2

enter stage assistants, set up rustic gate and zigzag fence, retire through sliding door

enter Kogo, enter maidservant, young-woman masks, sumptuous orange robes

sit

enter landlady, long blue robe, no mask, long white headdress, rasping sing-song speech, opens gate, speaks, closes gate, long slender fingers

Kogo and maid turn towards each other slowly, voices muffled by their masks, drummers pick up their drums, plok plik PLOK

musicians growl, intermittent drum beats, flute begins then stops, muffled voices from behind masks, landlady withdraws through sliding door, flute shrills, slowly Kogo and maid turn, face to front of stage again

drum
flute
voice

enter Nakakuni, white socks, gliding walk, bulbous blue-gold costume, speaks chantingly to the musicians' chant and drums chorus pick up fans, eight voices belly song, Nakakuni approaches gate, chorus put down fans, Nakakuni speaks, Kogo answers, maid stands, opens gate, returns and sits, Nakakuni steps to gate

Kogo speaks, Nakakuni recoils from gate

voice
drum
flute

Nakakuni sits by pillar

enter stage assistants, fold up fence, remove it, remove gate, adjust Nakakuni's costume, exit through sliding door

Nakakuni to centre stage, bows, speaks, opens fan, places letter on fan, approaches Kogo, kneels, presents letter, withdraws, Kogo reads letter

voice
drum
flute

Nakakuni turns towards front of stage, adjusts one sleeve, adjusts the other, kneels

breathing

Nakakuni rotates, infinite slowness, to face Kogo, looks, rotates with infinite slowness back again

flute
voice
drum

silence

Nakakuni stands, picks up fan, Kogo places letter on fan, Nakakuni withdraws, puts letter in clothing, slow dance, flute and drum, gliding diagonal steps, sudden swirl of sleeves, slow opening of fan, sudden stamp of one foot, of other foot, further glidings, stamp STAMP

pause

Nakakuni speaks, chorus chants, Nakakuni departs from stage, reaches curtain, whirls and stamps, shrill of flute

Kogo rises to her feet, stands, leans forward, no movement, looks

The Old Man of Shimo-Ochiai

got slowly off
the bus
bent in his brown

suit almost double
with age and
rheumatism into

a mark of
interrogation
of the pavement

from which
he picked a
cigarette

end he threw
with impatience
into the roadside

shrubs

Air

> *wherever you turn*
> *you are surrounded by language*
> *like the air*
>   John James

of course there are problems
such as being able to ask the way but not
being able to understand the answer

and people
in the trauma of having to speak to a
foreigner
sometimes freeze into a statue named 'Panic'

but in trains I pass the time
trying to pick my way through the adverts
spiky katakana, thickets of kanji
the looped lianas of graceful hiragana

in bars and restaurants
I am an inscrutable but baffled eavesdropper

but mostly I thread the trails of the city
carrying my own language in my head
carefully
like a pitcher of water brought
from a great distance without spilling a drop

taking care to maintain that balance
breathing an alien air

空気

もちろん　不自由もある
道が訊けても
答えが聞き取れない

とか　ガイジンに
話しかけられて　ニホンジンが
「パニック」という石仏に
姿を変える　とか

でも　電車に乗れば
片仮名のトゲトゲ
鬱蒼とした漢字
しなやかな平仮名の蔓を分けて
当てもなく中吊りの
茂みを散策

レストランや居酒屋では
おかしなスパイになる
正体を知られず　わけも
分からずに　盗み聞きして

けれど　それよりも
街のもつれた道々を
辿っているときが多い
ゆっくりと
遠くから頭にのせて運んできた
いっぱいの水差しのような
自分の言葉を
一滴もこぼさず

バランスをくずさないよう
気をつけながら　わたしは
不可解な空気を吸っている

translated by Arthur Binard

Some Cultural Uncertainties

Mr and Mrs Takasaki live next door
they speak no English I speak no Japanese
we meet on the path
and laugh and wave our hands about
and bow profusely at every juncture

although of course

    one
    never
    knows

a gaffe that in some other country might produce
a blood feud lasting generations
will here just possibly lead to

a barely perceptible
                widening
                            of the
                                          eyes

    one hair
    on the head
    of the universe
    out of place

and the whole damn thing will never work again

A Small Bestiary

the poetry of the carrier bag

Elephant

elephant dum
is a popular with us
he makes us feel dancing
like a conjuring trick

Penguin

her voice
was soft and beautiful
an excellent thing in a penguin

Rabbit

the touchy rabbit
jumped out of the peppermint field
don't puff out your cheeks so much
or you'll be balloons

Bon-Odori in Kabukicho

in a concrete square under floodlights
to the beat of three drummers on a scaffolding platform
to a melody repeated from crackling loudspeakers
the old women in their summer kimonos are dancing
circling and circling the makeshift stage

>step forward, step back
>hands sketch a rooftop in air
>hands make a small turning-inside-out gesture
>hands held up, palms facing each other
>clap clap clap-clap clap
>step forward
>step back
>a little dip of the body
>steady, graceful and tireless

on littered tarmac surrounded by concrete
under neon signs and posters of half-naked women
in the parish of gangsters and hucksters and pimps
they're dancing to welcome the revisiting dead

the old women in their immaculate kimonos
their hair done up neatly in buns
their faces without expression

Changing, Unchanged

in the small town by the sea
concrete has replaced weathered wood
and a car park has been built on the fishermen's dock
but the old temple still maintains its gravitas

shady paths newly gravelled and fenced
young pine trees planted amongst venerable cedars
but in the caves carved in the sandstone cliff
past pieties still sing in the silence

the garden is turning towards autumn –
a maple tree with one red branch
a faded lawn, a rectangular bed of yellowing reeds
a brisk wind ruffling evergreen bushes

as it scrambles uphill to the abbot's quarters –
and at the back of all this an eroding cliff
from an era long before temples and gardens:
geology fringed with dark hanging pines

in the museum the metamorphosis of a tree trunk
untouched but for two small faces carved in it
someone saw Kannon and child in a tree stump
incised a few notches and, wonderfully, left it at that

also, a bronze mirror
circular on its wooden base
clouded with patina, reflecting nothing
the full moon rising from a carved sea of clouds

Bow, Clap Twice, and Pray

wooded hills, rice fields and rain
a *torii*, and then a gravel path through trees

leading to a vermilion shrine and its three
objects of veneration, found, not made

a tree trunk forked at the base
with a notch where the wood divides

the torso of a hollow tree, an oval orifice
where a branch once grew

and an empty trunk curved smoothly around
the convolutions of its own interior

here, in a silence without contrivance
in the spacious quietness of this place

a generous spirit suggests her presence
tutelar of the blood-warm folded darkness

in which bone coalesces, eyeball swims to shape
and flesh reaches out to be small fingers

a woman, thirty-five or forty years old
walks with quick steps across the gravel

passing the souvenir shop outside the gate
(videos, vibrators and condoms

blow-up dolls, their mouths agape
in see-through plastic packaging)

throws a coin into the slatted box
bows, claps twice, and prays

Hokokuji

1

swept tarmac, just-so houses
manicured gardens
        (they must have combed that moss)
trimmed hedge and bamboo fence

river in its concrete channel
rinsing and smoothing shaggy green weeds

carp drift and play against the current
orange backs arching into sunlight

we stroll up the hill
        in crisp new light
to a wooden temple gateway

2

wave pattern in raked sand
very particular pine trees
we climb stone steps to the hall

a fume of incense, a seated Buddha
lacquer, gold, a clutter of objects for holy use
and two unwavering candle flames

the garden is river-boulders, pine trees, moss

and a sort of elongated red cabbage
        planted here and there
in a whiteness of abstract gravel

        sublime nonsense
        asymmetrical exactness

boundless space in a few square feet

3

we sit on straw mats
by the open sliding doors
to catch the faint cool breeze

        wooden steps
        straw-wrapped pine tree

        dark bamboo grove
        a smoke of grey-green light

Suzuki-san crouches down outside
attending to his camera
while his party assembles in readiness for

    click!

the formal record of their visit

The Way of Tea

> wabi *is that incompleteness which in fact contains no thought of incompleteness*
> Sen Sotan: *Zencharoku*

a small hut in the shadow of a bamboo grove or among trees

mountains and rivers transplanted to your fireside

lay in charcoal and hang a kettle over it

restore the heart with old tea utensils

listen to the water in the kettle sing like the wind in the pines

watch the four seasons pass in a few square feet

let the waves of the river Wei flow from the dipper

draw straight from the source of heaven and earth

savour in your mouth the taste of the wind

Kagekiyo

1

*sleeping on wet grass
a far estuary our destination*

*rowing across the sea
a city of clouds in our dreams*

*late dewdrops waiting
for the morning wind to blow*

2

blindness all blindness
one unending profitless darkness

a pine-bough hovel
a thin coat against the winter winds
my body a framework of bones

> *listen
> listen now to the wind
> the wind in the pine trees on the hill
> snow is coming
> snow*

why must I wake from dreams
of flowers I cannot see?

listen
listen now to the waves
the waves running
over rough stones to the cliff
the evening tide is in

my eyes cannot see autumn
but the wind brings news of a vanished past

3

they have beaten us in the mountains
and beaten us among the islands
and put us to flight at the passes –
how shall we defeat these Genji?

I landed alone on the beach
their massed ranks fled from my anger
how easy this killing is!
'I am Kagekiyo, captain of the Hei!'

sword points
and wild laughter on the battlefield

4

I am an old man
I have forgotten unforgettable things
a dragon grown old, outrun by village nags

my daughter
my daughter who never knew me
return to your home
my daughter, candle to my darkness
go on with your journey

>   *sleeping on wet grass*
>   *rowing across the sea*
>
>   *distant river mouth*
>   *city of clouds*
>
>   *late dewdrops waiting*
>   *for the morning wind to blow*

Hiroshima

1

The bomb fell rapidly and exploded after 43 seconds at an altitude of 580 metres. The blast stripped off clothing, tore off skin, and caused the rupture and explosion of intestines and other internal organs.

Wooden buildings within a radius of 2.3 kilometres were obliterated while those within 3.2 kilometres were half destroyed. Many people were trapped under their collapsed houses and were burned to death.

2

the grandeur of that cloud
        boiling up from the planet
in the morning sunlight

the hunger for apotheosis
for the obliterating suddenness of the flash

    I am become death, destroyer of worlds

as though
it would not be our own flesh which burnt

'when I took hold of her hand her skin came off like a glove'

3

'the professor
was standing by the tram tracks near Miyuki Bridge
he was almost naked
      clad only in his underpants
and was holding a rice ball in his right hand

beyond the tracks
the northern part of the city was a sea of fire

how
just then
and so many miles from his home
had he come to be holding a rice ball?

at that moment
he seemed a symbol of all
the modest aspirations of humankind'

From the Train

Grey roofs, blue roofs, red roofs, as far as the eye can see in morning sunlight. A twenty-year stubble of TV aerials. Concrete and wood-frame and prefabricated panel, and aluminium-railed balconies where bright bedding is displayed to sun and air. How many shades of grey can you see, grey-white and white-grey, flecked with bits of green: a blurred wisp of bamboo, a stroke of pine, a smudge of bush, a speck of rooftop bonsai. Here the adolescent ungainliness of a northern palm tree, there an evergreen bush clipped to a disciplined roundness; or a pine tree with straw knee bandages, its limbs racked and bound on a frame of bamboo poles.

Trains passing over and under trains, at tangents, at right-angles, stitching the fabric of Tokyo; trains vanishing out of the corner of the eye beneath the strict entanglements of the power lines; trains bearing the providers to their sites of loyalty, attrition, and the wherewithal to live.

Ifu Beach, Kumejima

1

shoreline waters glittering in sunlight
sea-heron stalking the shallows
a flock of dunlin running at sea's edge
a nimble flight of terns

skein of flickering wings
water's thin glaze over sand and reef and stone

2

eyes down to search for tokens
loving this shell and this one and this one

the grace of these anonymous sarcophagi
each an emblem
       of a life's urgent spiralling to order
licked clean by the sea's salt tongue
haunted by echoes, empty as light

3

twisted swordfish at the tide-line
fish corpses putrescent among driftwood
huge deadweight of a turtle

flippers spread-eagled
burst black eyes
tangled entrails
black blood encrusting the sand

its flesh
leaking out into nothingness
from the great flaking dome of its shell

4

a hermit crab walks past my feet
travelling for miles across a few yards of sand

it walks precisely on its toes
calciferous bundle on its back
having (it seems) a good enough idea of where it's going
overcoming all obstacles
surmounting driftwood and tangles of seaweed
persistent inheritor
purposeful migrant from pool to pool

walking the sea's edge in daylight

III

later

Vacuum Storm

haiku by Natsuishi Ban'ya

that's my brain there
that gap between
those fleecy clouds

bare branches
tonight again the constellations
are full of misprints

cherry blossoms falling
newsprint drinks
great draughts of human blood

into the Sea of Japan
the lightning's tail
is plunged

rainbow
raise your leg
over the Sea of Japan

pushed off the stairs
falling
I become a rainbow

diarrhoea
shitting electric wires, birds, fireworks
and clouds

sandstorm
head blown into
innumerable slopes

sometimes vacuums
sometimes clouds
pass through the lachrymal gland

the wind from the future
arrives
to cut the waterfall in two

over the gravestone shop
on the department store roof
radio waves fly

leaving the house
for a thousand years
at the door I hang a waterfall

the mountain range has ears
in the night
a stone is thrown

The Old Lady of Ogikubo

every time
I see her
in the

shopping street
very old
moving

very slow
bent double
over

her walking stick
good
I think

and greet her
still alive

Language Acquisition

my name is Pat
my field is language acquisition
and I'm trying to find out
how Japanese children acquire directives

I have lots of data
and there are a number of frequent patterns

for example
when a mother requests an action by a child
it usually comes with a reason why the child should comply

> *because that's the way things are done*
> *because Mother wants you to do it*
> *because people will make fun of you if you don't*

now I'm in a living room
and Aki-chan is eating a *mikan*, a Japanese orange
and her mother says: *Patricia-san says 'I want some too'*

I've said no such thing

Aki-chan
the not-deaf child
studies me carefully from under her fringe

then holds out the *mikan* towards me

Sashimi and Roses

delicate red chunks of raw fish
nestling on a cumulus of white crunchy daikon

a tiny mound of green mustard
one green leaf

the discretion of white-wood chopsticks

    ocean-borne scent
    salt and sword-edge and pine forest

sparseness and pale scrubbed wood
a slender vase with three red roses

and beneath it all

    the almost perceptible
    shifting of tectonic plates

(but you're not supposed to think about that)

刺身と薔薇

デリケートな赤身が
重なり合い　刻まれた大根の
入道雲の上に横たわる

　　　　山葵のひと山
　　　　一枚の緑の葉

箸の木肌はつつましく
　　　海風がほのかに匂う
　　　波の花　刃先　松の木々

洗われ　磨かれた卓上の
広やかさ

ほっそりしたガラスの花瓶には
真紅の薔薇　三輪

そして下の方　ずっと
　　　地中深く　岩石層の
　　　大陸プレートが微かにずれて

(しかしそれについては
考えなくてよいことになっている)

translated by Arthur Binard & Kisaka Ryo

A Letter from Ishinomaki

acres almost cleared of wreckage
here and there a building standing

blank stares of empty window-frames
a wall-less kitchen, a lampshade swinging in the wind
smashed machinery in a burst-open workshop
dislodged girders and loose wires dangling

a fishing boat on its side fifty yards from the sea

we're clearing a plot
of all the small things left behind by the crane

> video cassette (*The Twilight Samurai*)
> audio cassette (indecipherable)
> fragment of a broken CD (pink, indecipherable)
> nameplate (Nakamura)
> rusted kitchen knives
> broken blue crockery
> an elementary student's plastic ruler
> a tube of ketchup

When a plot's been completely cleared, it's sterilised with a white disinfectant powder; the homeless cats who have outlived their owners walk across it and then wash their paws, which will make them sick.

> *the tsunami was finally stopped*
> *by that wooded hill over there beyond the high school*
> *the first job the next day*
> *was to disentangle the bodies from the branches*

the post office is wrecked
but not the red-painted post-box on its stout single leg –
a car approaches along the pot-holed road
and stops: a woman rolls down the window
leans out and posts a letter

17-18 *December* 2011

An Unseen Crow

crust of earth
lifted by frost
on stems of fluted ice

cold platform
huddled pigeon
loudspeaker crackling

shopping street music
concerto for flute
and pneumatic drill

red light quiets
six lanes of traffic
an unseen crow caws

smell of sawn timber
sunny lunch-break
carpenters sit and smoke

見えない鴉一羽

(from the English . . .)

縦溝模様の氷の茎に
霜で持ち上げられた
地球のかさぶた

寒いプラットホーム
うずくまる鳩
拡声器パチパチ

ショッピング街の音楽
フルート協奏曲
と空気ドリル

赤い光静まる
六車線
見えない鴉一羽鳴く

のこぎり屑のにおい
ひなたの昼飯
大工たち座って喫煙

translated by Natsuishi Ban'ya

Notes

Notes

The earliest piece here ('Basho') was written in London early in 1969, when I had no idea that I would ever visit Japan; the other two poems in Part I were composed later that year during a six-month stay in Tokyo. 'Tokyo: Week One' dates from September 1981, when I arrived in Tokyo for a second time. The most recent poems are 'A Letter from Ishinomaki', which was written in the aftermath of the tsunami of March 2011, and the five haiku in 'An Unseen Crow', written (and translated by Natsuishi Ban'ya) in 2013.

Throughout the book, Japanese names appear in the Japanese order, with the family name first.

❧

BASHO An 'imitation' of Matsuo Basho's *Genjuan no Fu* ('Prose Poem on the Unreal Dwelling'), loosely based on the translation by Donald Keene in his *Anthology of Japanese Literature: From the Earliest Era to the Mid-Nineteenth Century*.

TOKYO: WEEK ONE The third set of Chinese characters in fact read 'Itabashi Honcho', the name of a subway station in northern Tokyo. Abe Kobo: *The Woman of the Dunes*. 'A world of signs without fault, without truth and without origin': Jacques Derrida, 'Structure, Sign, and Play' in *Writing and Difference* (translated by Alan Bass, 1978).

KOMACHI Ohta Shogo's *Komachi Fuden* ('Komachi as told by the wind') is a modern adaptation of the No play *Sotoba Komachi* by Kan'ami Kiyotsugu (1333–1384). The protagonist of both plays is Ono no Komachi, a Heian-period poet equally famous for her poetry, her beauty and her heartlessness. One suitor was refused until he should complete a vigil outside her house every night for a hundred nights. He died on the ninety-ninth night, but when Komachi was an old woman, he came back to haunt her; the climax of Kan'ami's play is a dance in which she is seized by his spirit and dances out his passion and grief. *Sotoba*: a stupa (a round structure erected as a Buddhist shrine).

KOGO: SCENE 2   The second scene of a No play by Komparu Zenchiku (1405–1468). The letter brought by Nakakuni is a love letter from the Emperor.

AIR   Epigraph: John James, *A Theory of Poetry* (Street Editions, 1977). Kanji (Chinese characters), hiragana and katakana (two different syllabaries) together comprise the writing system of the Japanese language.

BON-ODORI IN KABUKICHO   Bon-odori is the traditional dance of the festival of O-Bon, in which every August the spirits of the dead revisit the earth and are welcomed by their descendants; Kabukicho is a large red-light district in Tokyo.

BOW, CLAP TWICE, AND PRAY   The traditional manner of address to the spirit of a Shinto shrine. *Torii*: the gate at the entrance to the sacred precincts of a shrine.

THE WAY OF TEA   Sentences from *Chatei no Ki* (Teahouse Record) by Takuan Soho (1573-1645).

KAGEKIYO   Based on the No play attributed to Zeami Motokiyo (1363-1443); the complete play has been translated by both Ezra Pound and Arthur Waley. Kagekiyo was a captain of the Taira clan in the Genpei War of 1180-1185 between the Minamoto (Genji) and Taira (Heike) clans. After the defeat of the Taira, he was exiled to a remote area and subsisted as a blind old beggar. His daughter, who is searching for him, comes to his hut by chance and asks for directions, but, ashamed of his wretched state, he sends her away without revealing who he is. However, a villager brings her back, and father and daughter are briefly reunited. He agrees to tell her about his past as a warrior, but insists that after that his daughter leave him and return home.

HIROSHIMA The source of Part 1 is the introduction to the catalogue accompanying a Hiroshima Peace Memorial Museum exhibition of art by survivors of the bombing; the words of two of these survivors are quoted at the end of Part 2 and in Part 3.

LANGUAGE ACQUISITION Based on an incident reported by the linguist Patricia Clancy in her chapter, 'The Acquisition of Communicative Style in Japanese,' in *Language Socialization Across Cultures* (ed. E. Schieffelin & E. Ochs, 1986).

❧

SOME JAPANESE PLACE NAMES: Shinjuku and Shibuya are major sub-centres of Tokyo; Shimo-Ochiai and Ogikubo are Tokyo suburbs; Zuisenji and Hokukuji are Buddhist temples in Kamakura; Kumejima is an island near Okinawa in the subtropical Ryukyu chain; Ishinomaki is one of the towns in northern Japan most damaged by the tsunami of March 2011.

www.ingramcontent.com/pod-product-compliance
Lightning Source LLC
Chambersburg PA
CBHW031213090426
42736CB00009B/903